Chrome

Janette Voski

Chrome Copyright © Janette Voski, 2023.
Published on 5 August 2023.

All rights reserved. No part of this book may be reproduced or transmitted in any form or by any means without written permission from the author.

ISBN: 978-0-6456900-1-9 (paperback)

Front and back cover image photography by Gelica Peralta, Copyright © 2023.
Cover image design by Janette Voski, Copyright © 2023.
Interior illustrations by Janette Voski, Copyright © 2023.

Also by Janette Voski

BONES

X

NEON SUN

Thank you

Baba
For being a great teacher, mechanic and dad.
For always telling me how to fix exactly what's wrong with my car by simply listening to the engine. I'll never forget the first time I drove my car home and parked it in the garage. That smile on your face is seared in my memory.

Minass
For always encouraging me to create, pursue and achieve.
For telling me to "just come up with a really good idea" for my next book. (Here it is.) For using trigonometry to make a glovebox for my car.
For being the *lighthouse keeper*.

Eph 2:10
2 Tim 1:7

God gave me a light that set a fire in my soul
Even when I burn out
He gave me more light to ignite again
So I light myself back up
Fire found in my hands
I'll use them to guide my steps at night
Keep you warm, like sunlight
Tearfully smile with this revelation
As He told me
He didn't just give me this gift to help you
He gave me this gift
To help me too.

Contents

Preface ⋯ 1
Introduction ⋯ 3

Lighthouse Keeper ⋯ 7
Gravity ⋯ 8
Signal ⋯ 9
Alive ⋯ 10
Petrol ⋯ 11
Contentment ⋯ 12
Raven ⋯ 13
Candy Apple ⋯ 14
Capture ⋯ 15
Organised Chaos ⋯ 16
Perspective ⋯ 17
My Own World ⋯ 18
Making History ⋯ 19
Artist ⋯ 20
Purpose ⋯ 21
Reverence ⋯ 22
Psalm ⋯ 23
Coffee ⋯ 24
Rare ⋯ 25
Friendships ⋯ 26
White Dress ⋯ 27
Angle ⋯ 28
Anticipate ⋯ 29
Paint ⋯ 30
Jesus ⋯ 31
Glossy ⋯ 32
Poetry ⋯ 33
I Might Be Lying ⋯ 34
Pray ⋯ 35
Gesture ⋯ 36
Take Care ⋯ 37
Passenger ⋯ 38

Keep Going ⋯ 39
Drive ⋯ 40
Kill Switch ⋯ 41
Brake Fluid ⋯ 42
Ocean Apart ⋯ 43
Details ⋯ 44
Neigh ⋯ 45
Chain Of Events ⋯ 46
War ⋯ 47
It's Mine ⋯ 48
Interesting ⋯ 49
Predictable ⋯ 50
Sunshine ⋯ 51
Classic Car ⋯ 52
Unforgettable ⋯ 53
Racing ⋯ 54
Live Loud ⋯ 55
Sober ⋯ 56
Compatibility ⋯ 57
Repeat ⋯ 58
Disco ⋯ 59
Sixties ⋯ 60
Rain ⋯ 61
Revelation ⋯ 62
Chrome ⋯ 63
1964.5 ⋯ 64
East Coast ⋯ 65
Restored ⋯ 66
Love ⋯ 67
Red Roses ⋯ 68
Goodbye ⋯ 69

Preface

Chrome is a decorative piece found on motor vehicles, designed to be visually appealing. The polished surface of chrome shines like a mirror, reflecting light in the same way. To me, the perfect metaphor.

Sometimes we need only one moment of reflection to spark a revelation.

Here is a collection of mine.

Introduction

My first car was a silver late-nineties Holden Barina with a manual transmission. At the time, I knew only how to drive an automatic, so the first few days were interesting. My dad would hop in the passenger seat and get me to start the car, put it in gear and learn how to use the clutch. He never let me actually leave the parking spot and I never understood why. I didn't get far, literally. The first few times the car would bunny hop. I was adamant on learning how to drive a manual, and now that I had bought my car, didn't really have a choice.

After several times, I slowly began engaging the gear in time with the release of the clutch and the tap of the accelerator. Sometimes with a little shaking until the car stalled. Either way, each of these moments were met with the same enthusiasm and excitement. My dad didn't let me leave the parking spot until the first gear engaged like autopilot and the car hummed and moved forward as I accelerated. At this point, he said he was done teaching me, got out of the car, and left. A confused eighteen-year-old sat there in silence, before getting out, locking the doors and following him inside.

"Aren't we going to go around the block or something?"
"You already know how."

A couple of days later, I was supposed to head into the city. I asked my parents if they could drive me, and I'm sure my dad could have, but looking back, I know he just wanted me to have the trust in myself that he had, and the confidence to drive on my own. So, my shaky hands found the ignition and put the keys in, and I began my way into the city after a hopeful deep breath. I was getting the hang of it, until I was met with an amber-turning-red light on a little hill that felt like a steep mountain. I had to stop. The number of thoughts running through my mind could fill this page alone. I remember my trembling breath with the anticipation of the light turning green, but trying to keep it cool.

After the pedestrians crossed, I put it in gear and released the clutch. I ended up doing a burnout at one of the busiest intersections in Sydney – the corners of William and College Streets. I remember pedestrians laughing as I was too, but I was thrilled because I had made my first hill-start without stalling!

It's moments like these that led to my interest in eventually buying a classic. I would wonder what led others to own the cars they did – whether it was a necessity, a luxury, or both. I'd have these conversations momentarily with my dad, and he would talk about some of the better engines and cars he'd worked on. It was like having an encyclopaedia at my fingertips, but one that used colourful language to describe some of the worst cars to buy. Nevertheless, I appreciated how honest his responses were, "Nah, don't get that, you'll get x problem, it's very common", or "Yeah I worked on those, those are reliable".

With my interest in classic films peaking simultaneously, I began searching for a classic car. But not just any classic car. I was looking for American muscle. I had just watched *American Graffiti*. An American classic movie that felt like a goodbye to the innocence of adolescence. Though I am still young, the movie was reminiscent of the fear and hesitancy, even bittersweetness, that we all briefly share through that part of life. A wistful memory of perhaps your own life, realising that you're experiencing that too, or maybe you already have.

Along with the soundtrack, I loved the sense of excitement with the simple act of driving a car. It was like living to seek thrills, but them chasing you irrespectively. How much life is lived just by riding through the streets and how they connect us to the places we visit and the people we see. A blissful time capsule that you want to keep revisiting, of which you want to make your own.

So I did.

Contained in a pastel yellow painted piece of metal decorated with chrome, I bought a Phoenician yellow 1964.5 Ford Mustang. My own version of the blissful time capsule that was *American Graffiti*.

I began painting the city.

Chrome

Lighthouse Keeper

Just when the lighthouse keeper moved away
Just when I stopped my car on the shore
Wondering if I could swim or sink
Rust, combust or more.

Had to start back up
Drown the sounds and sores
Dip, ride and soar
Rattle, roar, ready for war.

Until I can stop with silence
Rest and restore
Get lost and find my way home
Until then, my only friend
My best friend made with chrome.

Chrome

Gravity

Feeling emotion forced by gravity
Engine grumbles before it rumbles
Ride's just as heavy.

Between the traffic lights
Empty streets
With my queued mind
Empty seats.

Impossible to be discreet
Like being on stage with blinding lights
Cue the heat, everybody looking at me.

Chrome

Signal

Old car, new memories
Single with accessories
Slow burn, good taste
No haste, slowly chased
Not looking, just driving around
Green light only allows the profound.

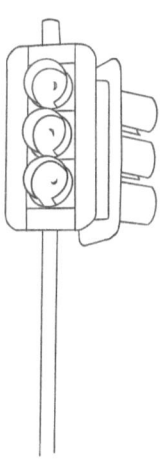

Chrome

Alive

A writer writes about it
A photographer takes its photo

Persistent in seeking beauty
Artists speaking second life
Into their muses, whatever they choose
One by inspired eyes
Driving like day one
Creating art to keep it alive.

Chrome

Petrol

Always fill up my own petrol
Get into yours empty
Where the fuel reaches the bottom
Where the tank is dirty.

Your burdens aren't heavy to bear
But you won't get far with no fuel in your car
So I siphon petrol for you
Just to fill yours up too.

You'll burn it up, you'll waste it away
You know I'll be here as long as you need me to stay.

Expense of petrol, priceless for you
Mine's always full. Fuel's easier to push but you pull.

Showed you how to fill up, showed you the line
That's when it'll click.
Robbery on the run
To be a good friend you must be willing to risk losing one.

Chrome

Contentment

Sometimes I go on drives that end up around North Sydney, on the borderline of Milsons Point and Kirribilli. Most of the time, it's autopilot. Even if I spent my time at Palm Beach, I'll somehow still end up there. I sit opposite the Opera House, watching the city light up and the harbour reflect its beauty, against the darkening sky. I begin to think, about many things. Particularly the friends I've made simply because of our cars. To have such different lives and lifestyles, maybe even live in different states or continents, yet hold the same appreciation, passion or interest in classic cars. For the sole reason that our paths have crossed, all because of a car...

And just like with any other relationship we form in our lives, at times, we meet some of these people only once, or twice. But if we're lucky, we manage to find some incredible friends within these opportunities that are presented to us.

With that thought, I smile.

Chrome

Raven

Raven black fastback
Dark features, light heart
Survivor like her GT
Driver oceans apart.

Raven black fastback
Shift gears, proceed en route
New bride, new life
Passion is her pursuit.

Raven black fastback
Timeless like a watch without a face
A 1967 driven in style
One never to be replaced.

Chrome

Candy Apple

Candy apple red with a cream top
Sounds sweet like a milkshake
Convertible got her hair windswept
Cruisin' thru the Golden Gate.

Candy apple red with a cream top
Reflections through the mirror ball
Hazy afternoon, sun sets soon
Rings around mountains to the wedding hall.

Candy apple red with a cream top
Timeless like a watch without a face
A 1967 driven in style
One never to be replaced.

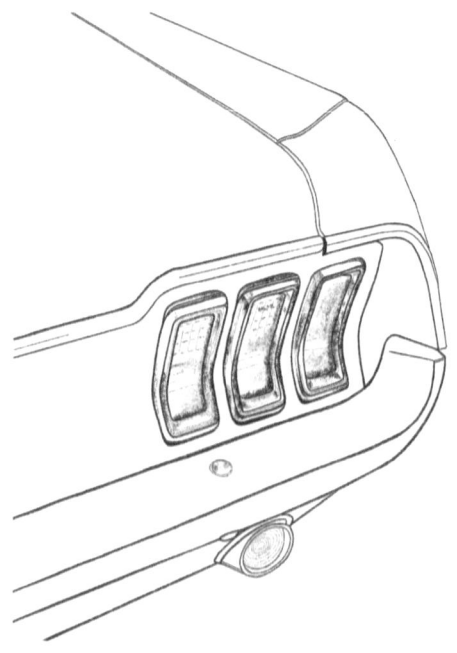

Chrome

Capture

Sometimes I wish I could capture a moment just by blinking my eyes
Sometimes I wish I could let you see through mine
Sometimes to remember it, I relive it but even the sunset differs each day
Reminiscing friends long gone, where memories begin to weigh
Sometimes I wish I could find how to slow down time
Sometimes, to see it again I close my eyes
It goes dark, as if I've been blinded by the flash like a spark
Sometimes, I wonder if we underestimate the power of reflection, where a smile turns into a laugh
Sometimes I wonder if we underestimate the impact of capturing a moment in a photograph.

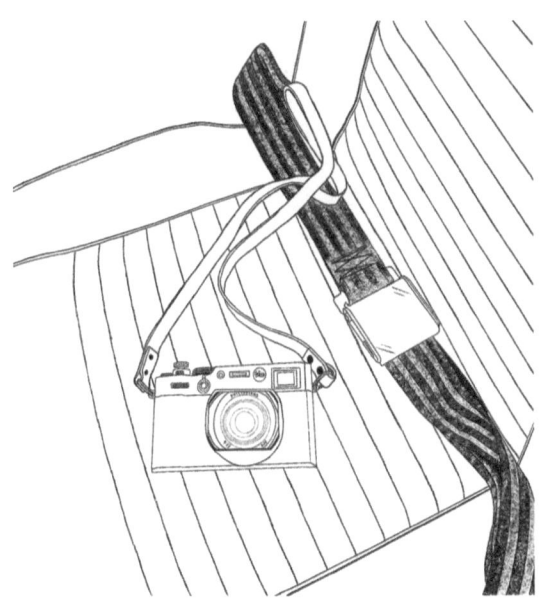

Chrome

Organised Chaos

I remember when my dash lights didn't work and neither did my horn. It wasn't long until I replaced my steering wheel but then ... still couldn't see. It was fine until the sun set but then it was great. Just playing a guessing game, reaching the same speed as the cars across the lane. Wondering what would happen if I get pulled over, convincing myself I could convince the officer. Used a speedometer app that tried to keep up with me but you can't cap something that just wants to be free. Come on, pony. Let's whistle, let's buckle! Don't worry darling, I'm confident as I half chuckle. Just let me enjoy your groaning and gloss for a little longer through the ride and night of my organised chaos.

Chrome

Perspective

Picture a classic car
Sitting in a wrecking yard
You would assume it is wrecked beyond repair.

Picture the same classic
Spinning in a museum
You would be certain it held well-founded value.

Chrome

My Own World

Noise pollution
Close the door
Sound resolution
Where the world is silent.

A world with four seats
Rapid beats
Turning corners
Cruising streets.

A world with gears
No fears
Can't outshine the coastline
But it shimmers like gold when it's mine.

Chrome

Making History

Dressing up for a mission
Dressing up to do nothing
Driving down the road
Feel my cheeks blushing

Cold starts, chrome hearts
Question marks, creating sparks

Dressing up for myself
Dressing up to make mystery
Driving down the road
Driven to make history.

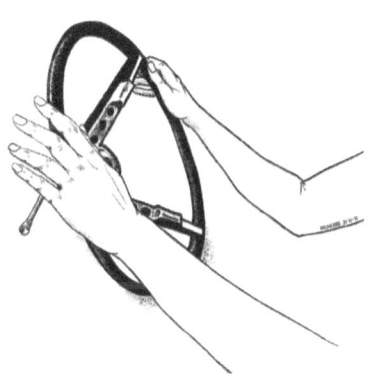

Chrome

Artist

Art that cannot be separated from the artist
Every letter an exhaled breath
Expressions of an overflowing heart, every coming apart
Letters creating words crafted into melody
Where every piece is a calculated part of me
Walk to my car, pop my bonnet
Rip something out of the engine bay, it doesn't run the same
Try to catch the ignition, it'll stall
I told you,
You can't take the artist out of this art at all.

Chrome

Purpose

Everybody's on their own clock, time doesn't run the same
Start sprinting to survive every day with an aim.

In this race, there's just one rule: don't wait to get left behind
The one-eyed man is king, in a world of the blind.

Target with tunnel vision, with no opponents
Your beating heart tells you you're meant to be in this moment.

This is your moment, a moment more
When every second isn't being counted but every moment is accounted for.

Chrome

Reverence

Don't trade deep connections for trivialities
Don't chase things that just shine
If you scrub something hard enough, and buff it up right
Anything could look divine.

Chrome

Psalm

Alluring mirage on the horizon, an illusion
Get closer as you lick your lips
Air's dry as your tongue
Thinking of just a sip.
Don't fall for the trap, keep driving
Thoughts running with your speed
But their illusions are deceptive
Why chase a reflection that disappears?
Dare to keep riding
It's not real, it's not real
Whisper to you, hoping you believe it
Dare to make a deal.
Turn away from empty promises
Turn away from roads where no roses grow
They offer nothing but hope and disappointment
So turn away and let it go.

Make it your mission, until navigation ends
Even then
Do it with nothing or your all
Look up
Fragrant lush garden, full of fruit
Fill your cup over from the waterfall.

Chrome

Coffee

Come, it'll be fun
Cruising
With a stop for coffee.

Stay, under the sun
Cruisy
Sipping my coffee.

Cars and coffee sounds great, but perhaps not this time.

Today, I think
I'll stick to my own rendition:
Classic, caffeine and my canine.

Chrome

Rare

Low supply, high demand.
Where you'll find value and no assets depreciate. Seek and you shall find it, whether you're against or behind it. Your vision in precision, causing coalescence, not collision.

Low expectations, high standards.
Where you've found value and peace of mind. Where some have it and others seek to find.

Chrome

Friendships

Friendships found and bound
Sounds of laughter all around
Even sitting in traffic.

Chrome cars, underground bars
Writing musings and memoirs, under sparkling stars
Like living in a classic.

Chrome

White Dress

Get the right ratio of fuel to air
Figure out if it's fitting
Feel at ease, feel wind in my hair
White dress sure is sitting

Scent of fuel, scent of fantasy
Higher than elation, not for everyone
Feel the breeze, feel reality
High hopes with the lowering sun

Violet sky turns blue-black
Pastel car, gold gradient
Plum lips turn to lip smack
White dress, bold statement.

Chrome

Angle

Under the blue moon, under cool lights
Passenger on the left but the driver's always right
When it's destined, risk and reward, there's no real gamble
No need to pick sides when it looks this good at any angle.

Chrome

Anticipate

I was at a roundabout
Lady didn't use blinkers
Hesitated with hands hovering over my horn
Maybe she didn't have fingers.

I was on the motorway
Car cut in front, mine begins to hum
Slammed brakes with both my feet
Yours hydraulic, mine disc and drum.

I was in my driveway
Sat for a little before the drive
Need to think three, maybe ten steps ahead
Anything can be a close call to survive.

Every time I go for a cruise
Apologise to my co-pilot, can't conversate
Every eye on my car, yet my eyes scan everywhere
Always have to anticipate.

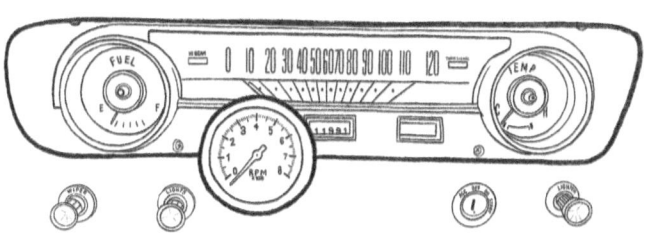

Chrome

Paint

If you ever get in my car, I'll always open the door for you.
I'll make sure your entrance is easy and free as the door can swing
I might be courteous but truthfully
I'm just being careful
Because the only time I ever damaged my car, it wasn't even me
Someone swung the door, it hit the kerb and I had the serenity of a saint
I don't want you to scratch the paint.

Chrome

Jesus

The thief of joy runs rampant
Don't let the enemy win
Focus on your radiance
That is power from within.

Let Him guide you
Call on His name
He holds the storm
With one breath, creates wind and flame.

You are special simply because you exist
With history and a story to tell, your own road ahead
Pour your heart, give it a start
But please don't burn your tread.

Chrome

Glossy

She likes shiny things
Admiring her glossy machine.
Glistens in the sunlight, gleams at night
Cleaned and sheened
Distributing delight in dopamine.

Chrome

Poetry

Beautiful yet intense, like driving poetry
Makes you feel something
Even in solitary.

Chrome

I Might Be Lying

Have you ever put your car in neutral just to hear it roar
So you rev it a little?

Have you ever sat in traffic watching the fuel or temperature gauge
Feeling your own temperature rising?

Have you ever looked at your reflection in a shop window
Just to see your car from another angle?

Have you ever found an isolated parking space
Just to see a herd around your car when you get back?

Nah ... me neither.

Chrome

Pray

Pray before ignition
Foot pushes lead
Pray during transmission
Safe ride ahead.

Chrome

Gesture

Drive by another classic, do a mini wave
My, my, how pure our hearts can be

How much a small gesture makes my day.

Chrome

Take Care

Take care of the people in your life.

They may feel like
        their fuel is nearing empty
        their ignition won't catch ...
But they'll look like they still run the same.

Check their temperature, replenish what lacks
When time rolls past slow yet fast
Do whatever it takes
To make them last.

Chrome

Passenger

Sit back, slink into the backseat
Crucial for mind, spirit and soul
Sometimes we must surrender control.

Chrome

Keep Going

There was a time when each ride was met with sadness, a longing for a passenger long gone. Over time, as with any other thing I've missed, the constant was my growth all along.

Chrome

Drive

Clink, jingle, crank. In go the keys
Engine rumbles, what a roar
Whisper apologies to the neighbours
As my foot taps a little more.

Sit for a minute, and maybe another
Sign my initials for the drive
Drop the handbrake as my lips lift
Caffeine free, feel revived.

Drive with no doubts
Drive with no regrets
Drive until the fuel runs out
Drive until the sun sets.

Chrome

Kill Switch

Stalled at the lights
What just happened? Is there a glitch?
Traffic builds up behind me
No hazard lights, just a hazard, a hitch
Lights turn green, I wave to the car behind me
Apologetically like a twitch
Cars swerving around me, as I look back down
Oh ...
I forgot to use the kill switch.

Chrome

Brake Fluid

Feels like an unspoken rule
I start my car, let it run idle
Dad meets me out the front
"We need to fix that rattle"
"And don't drive fast, it's been raining"
Competing with the sound of the engine to get a word in

Reversed down my driveway
Put my foot on the brakes
If the brakes are working, they're not
Foot forcing itself in fits to the floor
Crisp winter's day sure feeling hot

What am I going to do?
Thinking so much I think I forgot how to breathe
As he gestures "What's wrong with you?!"

Why are my brakes hitting the metal?
Thank God no one's behind me
Excitement turned more than unsettled

Turned the steering wheel
Backed into my neighbour's driveway
Slope forced my car to stop

Put it in gear as my body trembles with fear
Perhaps adrenaline, I slowly ascend back home
He places bricks behind my tyres
If I were in his field, I know I'd be fired
Turned the engine off, it felt as if it was a bad dream
But my dreams are never lucid...

He popped the bonnet and asked me
When did you last check your brake fluid?

Chrome

Ocean Apart

A classic from across the Pacific
Across the waves to your home
Heart full of the arts, chrome and commitment
With passion full of vibrant pigment

Met through familiar scent of fuel and friendship
Yet every bit was new

Had we never bought our cars
I wonder how our lives would differ
From such a distance afar.

Chrome

Details

No airbags, just lap belts
What a time to be alive
1964 to 2023
Such history survived

No sensors, just senses
Much changed over the years
Still appreciate its class, its beauty
Why buyers are met with seller's tears

No seat warmers, just sit on the bonnet
No auto windows, just hand cranked and vented
No push to start, just pump the fuel
No new car smell, just fuel scented.

Chrome

Neigh

You want to hear a joke?

Two mustangs walk into a bar.
What did they ask the bartender?

Where to find a stable drink.

Chrome

Chain Of Events

At sixteen I got my learner's licence
Walked into class late
At seventeen I passed my driver's test
Instructor made me wait
At eighteen I bought my first car
Silver three-door hatch
At nineteen my interest in golden age films peaked
I watched a batch
At twenty I discovered fifties rock and roll
Pictured living through those times like *what if*
At twenty-one I sang to Lana Del Rey
Looking for more life to live
At twenty-two I bought my classic Ford Mustang
Found new life from fresh bliss
...
What a chain of events that led to this.

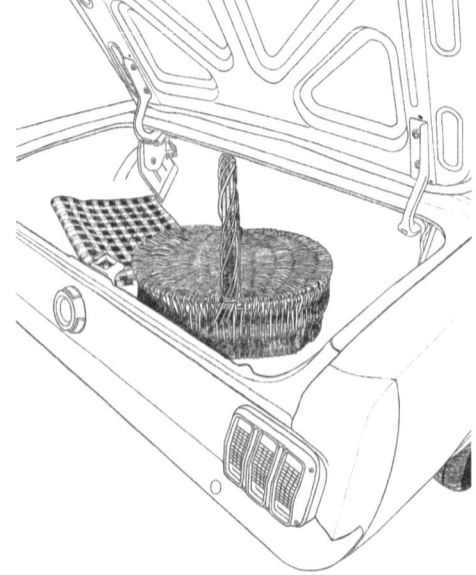

Chrome

War

Mind in deep thought
In for the long drive
Where burdens become obstacles
Road becomes the war in my mind.
Strategy is necessary when overcoming war
So much, some call it an art
The art of war, the war in mind
My only defence, my bumper bars.
Skill must be exerted
Driver's responsibility
Train your thoughts, not trust them
Moving with agility.
Charcoal foreground with yellow and white accents
When it's a force of nature, you don't fight
Like the sun reflecting onto the chrome, beaming into my eyes
Keep driving until bright light shines at midnight.
Humming rich history
Grumbling street names
Remaining dynamic
In a car that remains unchanged.

Chrome

It's Mine

Drive up to the petrol station
Need to fill up the car
People turn to glance
Oh, I know she's the star.

"Nice. Want to swap?"
"I'm good." Words elongate through my laugh.
"What engine? What year?"
"289, '64 and a half."

Just as I'm thinking of the next incline
"Is it your dad's?"

I turn to watch the pump fill up
No.
It's mine.

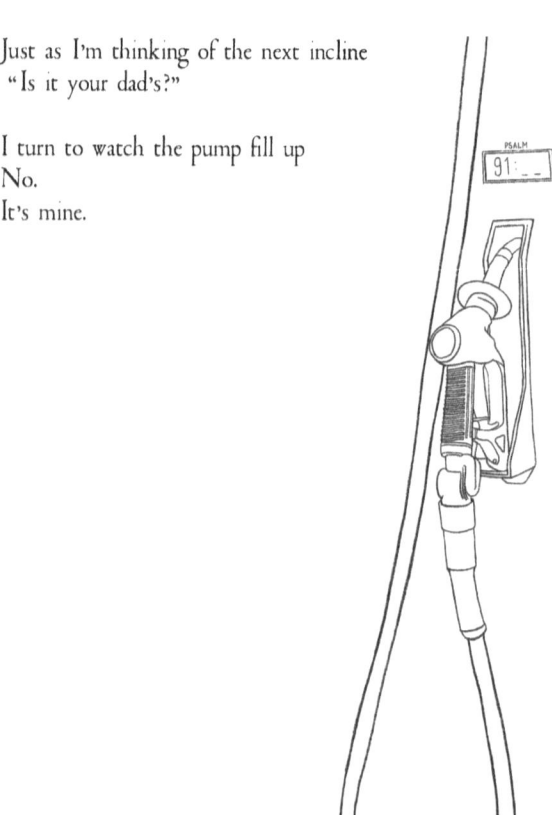

Chrome

Interesting

When I first got my car, Dad helped fix everything
That was my intention.
When I first got my car, Mum thought it was too noisy
Now she loves the sound of the engine.

In the winter time, engine warms the car up nicely
Like finding warmth in the thought of you.
Now I'm wondering why I don't get asked if it's my dad's when I drive his BMW.

Chrome

Predictable

It could be the sunniest, warmest day
Not a cloud in forecast
But as soon as I wash my car
That storm rolls in so fast.

Chrome

Sunshine

When I showed my mum the classic Ford Mustang ad
She said it was perfect for me
Because she calls me Sunshine.

That was when I knew that pony was mine.

Chrome

Classic Car

No mistaking it in car parks with that chrome everywhere. Just like its driver, it's got its own flair. Push the pedal a couple of times but not when the engine's hot. The right amount of wrong and you'll be stuck in the same spot. No bells, just whistles. So whistle along. But don't get in if you're light-headed; Mum tells me the fuel smells strong. I'll listen to its rattle, maybe turn on the radio. Just not at those drive-ins, my battery may not last the show. Who said they're not reliable when they consistently need service? Don't worry about that sound, am I making you nervous? Roar up a hill, tap it without trying. Undoubtedly every time, feel myself smiling. No stress, picked out my dress, I'm ready. No makeup when idling, it's not steady. Don't need to let you know when I'm outside, you can hear the engine rumbling when it's time to ride. Such power beneath this bonnet. It creates curvatures in lips and dust like a comet. Like a club versus a specialised whisky bar, you just can't beat a classic car.

Chrome

Unforgettable

Hot day, hotter engine, a little sweat
No threat detected, thoughts reflected
Call you chrome, hard to forget.

Chrome

Racing

Hard not to want to push the pedal when your life is falling apart
To feel in control of speed until the racing of your heart
Don't give up or lose hope, just count to ten
At least until you lose control again.
How can I be in so much pain yet feel so alive?
You only need to renew your mind on this drive
Eyes well up, like when wind is bracing
Now just your thoughts should be racing.

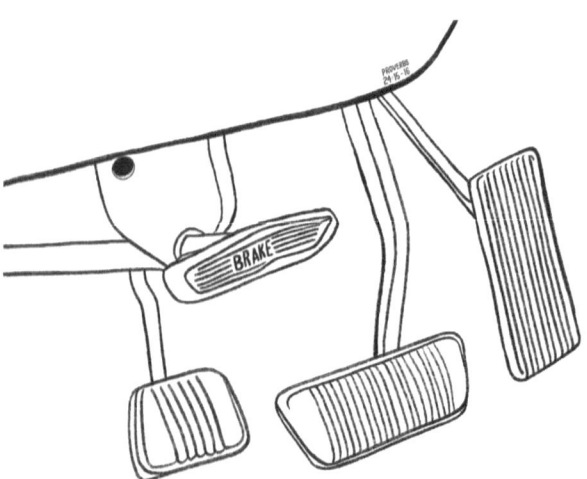

Chrome

Live Loud

Who said you're too old for adventure?
Who said you're too young for life?
If desire comes before acquire
Divine comes after strife.
Put the windows down
This is the youngest we'll ever be again
Get your temperature up
No harm in fun now and then.
In a world that wants my silence
I'll seek the lowest valley of every peak
Build stamina and endurance
With no breath left to speak.
Climb every hill, swerve around potholes
Feel suspension keeping me stable
Increased lung capacity, increasing speed
I'll shout out until I'm no longer able.

Chrome

Sober

Drive to the party
I don't even take a sip.
Everybody's getting tipsy
Only got serenity on my lips.

In my introversion I step outside for air
In reality, making sure my car's still there.

Come back to be greeted with joy
Same kind I feel on a ride
Beaming over the time when it's time to go
Just to be able to drive.

In my extraversion I share
If anyone needs a lift, I've got a spare.

Chrome

Compatibility

Maybe the globes aren't compatible
If your tail lights aren't working
And if your steering feels too hard
Remember to pump up your tyres.

My dad was talking about my car,
But I left feeling inspired.

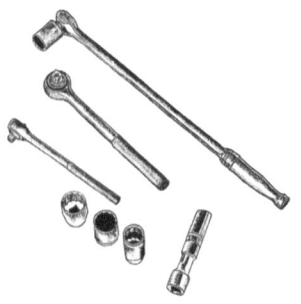

Chrome

Repeat

Where the road reaches moonlight
When the melody harmonised
Fresh air, energised

Went on a ride into the night and it led me to this road
Beneath the full moon
Stand still for a moment and take a breath
Look up and think of you

Chrome reflects a light I feel like I've consumed
Arms out like the waves at sea
Feet tapping, move to the beat
Harmony turns to hum
Surprise to you, no surprise to me
Just water, no spiced rum
Spin and giggle in my own company
Pray others find this contentment, this complete
As I reach to play the song on repeat

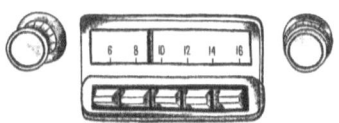

Chrome

Disco

Mirror ball hanging 'neath my rear-view mirror
Reflections too small for my view
Reflecting light into my disco interior
Mirroring my thoughts of you.

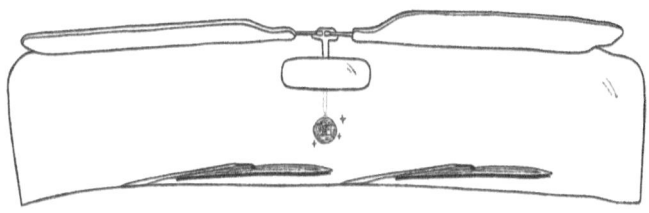

Chrome

Sixties

Pine for a life yet to be lived, like
Stepping into the sixties stylised.

If eyes are a window to the soul,
His, a door leading to warm sunshine.
Colour and sweetness of caramelised honey
Classic style, architecture and design.

Two cars and their headlights meet
Unsure of intent, makes them hesitate and retreat.
Slow and intentional manner but I wanted it static
Why must we both be enigmatic?

Timeless but stuck where seconds pass
Like driving and wanting the ride to last.

Passed each other.
Perhaps another time
In a life yet to be lived, I found you were mine.

Chrome

Rain

Driving in the rain
Headlights shining through droplets
Creating rainbows with hues like sage and champagne.

Chrome

Revelation

Rest my wrist out my window
Pen ready when my mind evokes
Curative while in limbo, words I wish I spoke

Painted nails like black cherries
Only bite when it's ripe
On the road to make your mind a weapon
Growth through a pen I snipe

I'm tired of shooting when I want to soar
No sweat, not a strain
When happiness is elusive
I've got perfect aim.

Chrome

Chrome

Come on, darling. Take me home
With that grumble and rumble edged in chrome.

Chrome

1964.5

There was nothing but the sound of the waves kissing the shore and the engine's explosive exhaust. The taste of sea salt on my tongue and the smell of pines, leather and fuel.

The sun came down to meet with the raspberry-glazed, lilac skies. I wanted to experience it in all its unfiltered, raw beauty. I pulled my sunglasses off and placed them in my lap. My eyes were burning but I didn't mind.

The engine heated the car like a hot summer's day, so I rolled the windows down and felt the wind through my hair.

My thoughts were running as fast as I was building speed. We glided downhill, swerved around bends and I felt the power of the throttle as the car soared uphill. It would shake and rattle whenever we came to a halt.

I didn't always know where I wanted to go, but that was part of the beauty. I just sought the thrill of an adventure.

Heads would turn, kids would point – but I was unaware. It felt like a timeless fantasy. As if I was dozing on the sand under the sun, dreaming of a day this enchanting. The moment itself was that intoxicating.

I never felt alone even when I was.

My foot heavy on the accelerator, stationary turned screeching
My very own pulse stimulator, speed limit, probable breaching.

Chrome

East Coast

On the east coast
Where the sun rises
On the west
Where it sets
Drive north for family
South for beaches
White sand where it's best
Ride along the ocean
Scan to see the sea glistening
Warm breeze singing duets
Look back to the road, the other cars
Smiles and gazing seem inviting
Watching the same spectacle in silhouettes.

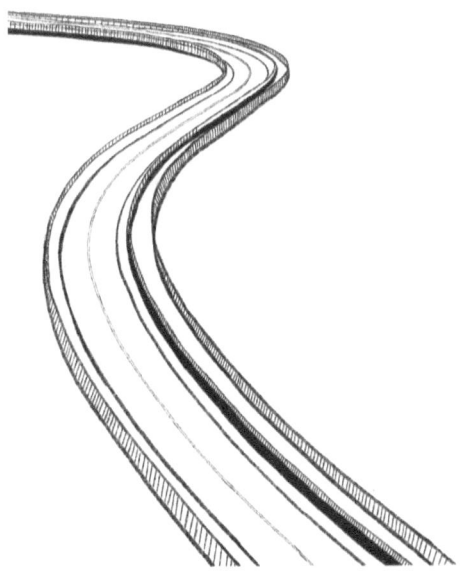

Chrome

Restored

I met with the same shore, heard it speak to me in waves
Wondering where next I'll roam.
I'm restored, stirred exactly how the sand craves
Was lost and found my way home.

Classics don't just appeal to one
Their class brings attention from most
But attention isn't always an invitation
Unless it comes in tireless waves from the coast.

Chrome

Love

Ambrosial scent overtakes the fuel and vinyl
Take my scarf from my neck to wrap my hair
Striking eyes, you're steadfast
Bask in the sunlight, warmth at last
Where nothing else exists in your eyes
Where perfect love drives out fear
Where thoughtful gaze exists and when afar, our hearts near.

Chrome

Red Roses

From one rose dipped in lacquer that lacked the beauty of its scent
To a bouquet rich with scarlet complexion and sweet accents.

Without my broken heart, with reanimated life of paradise
Seasons with reason, grains of salt, sugar and spice.

Lesson that led me to chrome, navigating to direct me home
Wind stirs, spices entice.

Every walk grown into love with intent
Red roses to my future and present.

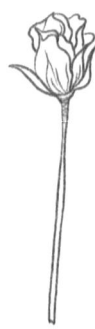

Chrome

Goodbye

Smell of petrol, smells like home
Never thought one of the oldest friends I had would be chrome
Tears on vinyl shoulders, met people I no longer know
Many chapters passed, the book's about to close
Time for me to go
Part of me doesn't want to, but I do think it's time
This moment of you will always be mine
Burned in my memory, every round and ups and downs
But I'd be lying if I said I enjoyed your every sound
Spoke to you in words, whistles and tears, you spoke to me in music
When your song was roars, shakes and rattles
Through my amusements and every battle
Fixed you, replaced pieces of you and made them new again
Had you for years, almost ten
Tug of war,
Wanting to ensure the next takes care of you as much as I
When they buy, and I wave bye, you'll still sing but
In my silence can't promise I won't cry
Then when I can't hear you sing anymore,
Tears hit concrete not vinyl
No room for denial, it'll feel final
Go on, make someone else happy now,
Make someone else's days and years
Never thought I'd ever say this, especially while fighting tears
I also never thought one of my oldest friends would be chrome
My journey with you is at its end,
But the next might just need a friend
One who's sleek, sings when they speak,
One who will drive them to their peak.

Special Mentions

Natasha
We connected over music and lyrics then realised both our hearts were full of poetry. Thank you for talking me out of selling my car every. single. time. and for your consistent display in loyalty.
I am grateful for you.

Michael
We met because you own the race car version of mine, but it is because of your good heart that we remained friends.
I am grateful for you.

Gelica
A poet behind the lens.
Each moment that led to you buying your cameras and Mustang was a blessing as it was a combination of these passions that led to our friendship.
I am grateful for you.

Nostalgic emphasis
Reminiscent.

Historic elegance
Eloquent.

@janettevoski

www.ingramcontent.com/pod-product-compliance
Lightning Source LLC
Chambersburg PA
CBHW020329010526
44107CB00054B/2038